With drawn

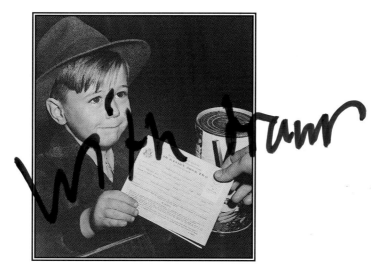

Children
of the
WORLD WAR II HOME FRONT

Children
of the
WORLD WAR II HOME FRONT

Sylvia Whitman

Carolrhoda Books, Inc./Minneapolis

To Nathaniel—may all your wars be pretend.

Front cover: A young boy uses war rations to buy tomato juice in 1943.
Page one: In 1942, a girl gathers rubber and metal for a scrap drive supporting the war effort.
Page two: Children in Fairfax County, Virginia, learn how to shop during wartime.
Opposite page: Members of the La Roe family of Austis, Florida, relax in the evening below portraits of family members serving in the war.

Text copyright © 2001 by Sylvia Whitman

Carolrhoda Books, Inc.
A division of Lerner Publishing Group
241 First Avenue North
Minneapolis, Minnesota 55401 U.S.A.

Website address: www.lernerbooks.com

LIBRARY OF CONGRESS CATALOGING-IN-PUBLICATION DATA

Whitman, Sylvia
    Children of the World War II home front / by Sylvia Whitman.
        p. cm. — (Picture the American past)
    Summary: Explores the experiences of children living in the United States during World War II, including writing V-mail to soldiers, participating in air raid drills, planting Victory Gardens, buying stamps for war bonds, and gathering cooking grease and scrap metal for making bombs.
    Includes bibliographical references and index.
    ISBN 1-57505-484-1 (lib. bdg. : alk. paper)
    1. World War, 1939–1945—Children—United States—Juvenile literature. 2. World War, 1939–1945—Children—Juvenile literature. 3. United States—Social conditions—1933–1945—Juvenile literature. 4. Children and war—United States—Juvenile literature. [1. World War, 1939–1945—United States.] I. Title. II. Series.
D810.C4 W458 2001
940.53′161—dc21   00-008615

Manufactured in the United States of America
1 2 3 4 5 6 – JR – 06 05 04 03 02 01

CONTENTS

Left: In the 1940s, before television became popular, most Americans listened to the radio for news and entertainment. Many first learned of the Japanese bombing that brought the United States into World War II from radio reports. Opposite page: Early in 1942, children at a San Francisco, California, elementary school say the pledge of allegiance to the flag.

Bombs Away

We are going to win the war . . .
and the peace that follows.
—President Franklin Delano Roosevelt, 1941

In 1941, Americans felt better than they had in years. Farm, bank, and business failures had led to hunger and poverty in the 1930s. But the hard times of the Great Depression were ending. Although people worried about a war overseas, battles helped business. Factories made guns and tanks. Americans had jobs.

December 7, 1941, was an ordinary Sunday. Children read comics, played tag, or ate family dinner after church. President Roosevelt worked on his stamp collection. Many people were listening to football or music on the radio when voices interrupted with terrible news. Japanese planes had bombed the Hawaiian port of Pearl Harbor.

Pearl Harbor, Hawaii. An American ship in flames sinks at a military base after an early morning attack by the Japanese on December 7, 1941.

The surprise attack on Pearl Harbor killed about three thousand sailors and citizens. It ruined 19 ships and 188 planes. It brought a faraway war to America's doorstep. In shock, Americans stayed tuned to the radio for more news.

A newsboy carries papers with headlines reporting the Japanese attack on Pearl Harbor. Angry over the attack, many Americans called the Japanese and Japanese Americans by the ugly nickname "Japs."

President Roosevelt asked Congress to declare war on Japan. Within days, the United States was also at war with Germany and Italy, Japan's partners.

Eleven-year-old Peggy Blassingame was scared. "I knew war meant people got killed."

Would the Japanese strike again? Rumors swirled. Children learned to identify planes overhead.

Many towns ordered blackouts so that enemy pilots would miss their targets at night. Street lamps stayed off. No one was supposed to light even a cigarette. People covered windows with black paper or curtains.

Washington, DC. Boys at Armstrong Technical High School make model airplanes to be used by the United States Navy in training.

Washington, DC. Volunteers go over plans for air raid drills, which helped people practice hiding from air attacks.

To prepare for a possible attack, Americans took part in air raid drills. Volunteers gave directions. Everyone hid. "The searchlights and sirens struck great fear in our hearts, and yet it was exciting," recalls Sheril Cunning. She and her sister stashed a catsup bottle in the closet. If enemy soldiers found them, they planned to glop on fake blood and play dead.

A soldier in uniform visits with friends and family.

Many Americans rushed to join the military. Others were drafted, or told by the government that they had to serve. Soon everyone knew a man or a woman in uniform.

Japanese American families suffered after Pearl Harbor. Many neighbors treated them like traitors.

Prejudice against Japanese Americans, two-thirds of whom were American citizens, drove many to post signs stating their loyalty to the United States.

Roosevelt allowed the army to move roughly 120,000 people of Japanese ancestry from the West Coast. They had to close stores and homes in a hurry. Each person could bring only one suitcase. Children had to give away toys and pets.

San Francisco, California. People sit near their packed belongings before being forced from their homes and moved to a relocation camp.

Manzanar, California. Japanese Americans spent most of the war at rough camps in the desert. The camps were sandy and hot. But children joined scout troops, played baseball, and even planted Victory Gardens.

The army moved Japanese families to relocation camps. Farmers, shopkeepers, nurses, teachers, students, moms, and lots of children found themselves ringed by guards and barbed wire. Yet they had done nothing wrong.

"You feel all tangled up inside," said one young man.

*New York, New York. Home on leave—a short vacation from military duty—
soldiers marry their sweethearts.*

Across the country, troops were training before shipping out for
Asia and Europe. The threat of death made people hungry for
life. Many soldiers quickly married their sweethearts and had
"good-bye babies."

A toddler tugs at his father's leg. Reunions during the war were short but sweet.

Homecomings were extra happy during World War II, and good-byes were extra sad.

Above: A mother says good-bye to her child before she joins other working women at her job at a defense plant.
Opposite page: Americans reminded each other not to complain about shortages. "Don't you know there's a war on?" they said.

"Don't You Know
There's a War On?"

Use it up, wear it out, make it do, or do without.
—World War II home front saying

Families on the home front followed the war through radio, newspapers, and newsreels—short films shown before movies. Early reports were grim. The German and Japanese armies fought fiercely. If an American was taken prisoner or badly hurt or killed, the War Department sent a telegram home. People dreaded those yellow envelopes.

The country felt different with so many dads, uncles, and brothers gone. Women were in charge at home. They fixed leaky sinks. They paid the bills. Some ran family farms.

Businesses couldn't find enough male workers. The government urged women to pitch in. Although many mothers had never worked outside the home, they put on pants, tied back their hair, and joined assembly lines. Factories churned out everything from bug spray to bullets. When one American ship sank, a sailor survived by clinging to the nearest life belt. It had been inspected by his own mom in Ohio.

Many American women worked in factories to help support the war effort.

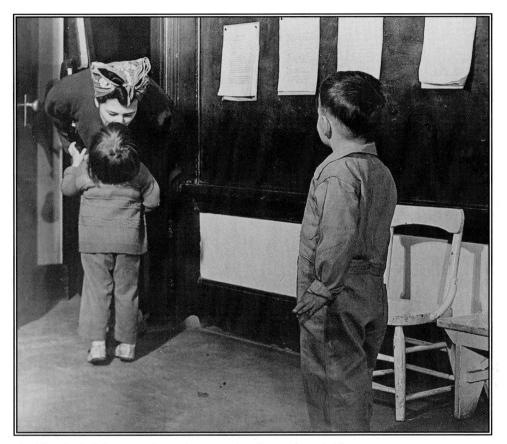

Oakland, California. A working mother leaves her child at a war nursery, or day-care center.

Children went to day care so moms could work. The government opened "war nurseries" and built cheap housing near factories. Many families moved to fill jobs making military equipment. Thousands of black Americans left the south to work in the north.

A number of states decided to ignore laws against child labor. By 1943, three million children, some as young as twelve, were working part-time.

Even young children worked during World War II.

Chicago, Illinois. Students saved dimes and quarters to buy $263,148.83 in bonds. The bonds helped the government build or buy 125 jeeps, two airplanes, and a motorcycle.

Americans supported the war in many ways. People who bought a bond for $18.75 could trade it in after ten years for $25. They were lending the government money. Children saved dimes to buy stamps, filling booklets until they had earned a whole bond.

Washington, DC. Sixth graders learn about the latest ration book from their teacher at Murch Elementary School.

To feed the army, the government rationed, or limited the supply of foods such as sugar, butter, beef, and canned goods. Every man, woman, and child on the home front was issued ration stamps by the government.

Two girls compare point values and prices for rationed canned goods at a grocery store. Rationing reminded one girl of the game Monopoly.

Grocers tagged food twice, with prices and with ration points. Shoppers needed both money and stamps worth a certain number of points. Families had to plan meals carefully. Shoes and gas were also rationed. Americans came to expect long lines and shortages of everything from tomato sauce to boots.

A few people secretly paid extra to shop without ration stamps. Most Americans didn't cheat. They wanted troops to have plenty of food, fuel, and shoe leather.

Families and schools grew backyard Victory Gardens. Children planted seeds, pulled weeds, and picked vegetables for dinner. Americans who ate homegrown beans and tomatoes didn't have to spend ration stamps on canned ones. What farmers grew could be canned and shipped to the battlefront.

San Francisco, California. A father helps his daughter and other Girl Scouts plant seedlings in a Victory Garden.

Washington, DC. A boy carries a pile of old sneakers and other rubber goods for recycling in his wagon.

    Factories needed raw materials, so people on the home front recycled. Melted down, one tire could make twelve gas masks. American children gave up sneakers, balls, and rubber dolls to support the war.

Roanoke, Virginia. On fat-collection day, children contribute the cooking fat each family has saved.

Mothers saved cooking fats, which factories used to make explosives. Bacon grease helped bombs explode.

Roanoke, Virginia. Scrap-metal drives were a common sight during World War II. Here the Junior Commandos of Roanoke pile on the metal.

Every community held scrap drives for leather, paper, string, and cloth. Metal was the most useful. Children collected tin cans, steel nails, aluminum foil, pots, even mattress springs. "Junk will win the war," sang a singer on the radio.

Children knew their work was important. "As all-American kids," one boy said, "we saw ourselves as good guys who were united against the bad."

Above: At the Granada Relocation Center in Amache, Colorado, Peggy and
Bobby Miyake and their mother gather around a picture of the children's father,
who is serving in the war.

Opposite page: Girls at Roosevelt High School in Los Angeles, California, practice
their aim with a rifle.

A Hard-Won Peace

More than an end to war,
we want an end to the beginnings of all wars.
—President Franklin Delano Roosevelt, 1945

The war years, from 1941 to 1945, seemed to last forever. Children grew up far from their fathers, uncles, and older brothers. Families kept in touch by writing. V-mail from the home front to soldiers cost only three cents. Letters circled the globe. But a piece of paper was no substitute for a hug.

As children grew up, many prepared to serve their country. They studied first aid and marksmanship (how to shoot guns) at school. One teenager at the time remembers "a good feeling, a believing in our country and our government, a sense of us all pulling together."

New soldiers, some just eighteen, left for the battlefront. The Germans had taken over much of Europe. But the United States and its friends—the Allies—were slowly driving them back.

On June 6, 1944, called D day, Allied troops stormed the beaches of France. People on the home front prayed for the safety and success of the soldiers.

New York, New York. Schoolchildren pray in support of the Allies during the D day invasion of France.

Just as the Allies were about to claim victory in Europe, President Roosevelt died. His health had crumbled under the weight of war. Many Americans felt as if they had lost a father. President Roosevelt had led the United States for twelve tough years. Children had known no other president. Sad citizens lined the streets and railroad tracks as Roosevelt's body traveled home.

Washington, DC. People line the streets of the capital during the funeral of President Roosevelt.

Less than one month after Roosevelt's death, in May 1945, the Germans surrendered. Church bells rang. But World War II was not over yet. Troops were still fighting in Asia. Many Americans expected a bloody invasion of Japan.

Chicago, Illinois. On V-E (Victory in Europe) Day, students celebrate victory and show support for the troops still fighting in Asia.

One American girl had nightmares for a week after watching newsreels of the atomic bomb blasts. She said it was as if "some kind of scary, terrible force had been set loose that nobody had any way to contain."

To prevent more battles, President Harry S. Truman decided to use a secret new weapon. In August, the United States dropped two atomic bombs on Japan.

Each bomb destroyed a city. No one had ever seen such fiery explosions before. About 140,000 men, women, and children died. Heat hotter than the sun burned the print of robes into people's skin. Many Japanese became sick from radiation.

Atomic bombs scared the whole world. They could destroy the planet. Some Americans criticized Truman's decision. But most were happy because the Japanese surrendered quickly.

On August 15, Americans celebrated victory over Japan and the end of World War II. People of all ages poured into the streets waving flags, throwing confetti, blowing whistles, dancing in fountains, even kissing strangers. The "good guys" had won.

New York, New York. In Times Square, crowds gather to celebrate Japan's agreement to surrender in August 1945.

A boy and his father, a disabled veteran, face the future together.

Returning troops packed into boats and trains. But veterans could not pick up their old lives as if nothing had happened. The country had changed. Soldiers had changed.

The horrors of war scarred minds as well as bodies. Nine-year-old James Covert expected his older brother to come home "joyful and happy and successful." Instead, "he was sad; he was hurt."

Osage, West Virginia. Swimmers pose in front of a swimming pool built as a memorial to local miners who died during World War II.

More than 410,000 Americans died in World War II. Children lost fathers and brothers, aunts and uncles. Communities built memorials. Families hoped no one would forget the men and women who laid down their lives to defend their country and their friends around the world.

Congress passed a law to help veterans and their families. Returning soldiers and sailors could borrow money to buy a house or open a business. They could attend college for free.

The children of the home front and their parents worked to rebuild their lives. Many families built new lives and homes, often moving to the suburbs, neighborhoods just outside cities.

Americans tried to put the war behind them. So many veterans married and had children that they caused a "baby boom." Families bought houses with grassy lawns where children could play. As shortages ended, factories returned to making sleds, skates, and toys. Birthday cakes had frosting again. Children looked forward to growing up in a land of peace and plenty.

WARTIME FOOD

A Recipe for Make-Do Cake

During the war, cooks on the home front had to make do or do without many of the usual ingredients in cakes and cookies. Factories used sugar to make alcohol that went into explosives. Its use at home was strictly rationed. Shortages and high prices for milk, butter, and eggs made these ingredients harder to find, too. But cooks made changes to their recipes to make do with non-rationed and more plentiful foods. This recipe for a spicy wartime cake could satisfy a sweet tooth while using less sugar than usual and leaving out eggs, butter, and milk.

Make-Do Cake

1 cup brown sugar, firmly packed

1 1/2 cups water

1/3 cup lard or other shortening

2 cups raisins

1/2 teaspoon ground nutmeg

2 teaspoons cinnamon

1/2 teaspoon ground cloves

1 teaspoon baking soda

2 tablespoons water

1 teaspoon salt

2 cups all-purpose flour

1 teaspoon baking powder

1. Preheat oven to 325° Fahrenheit. Take a bit of lard or shortening and grease the bottom and sides of an 8 x 8 x 2-inch baking pan. Sprinkle a tablespoon of flour inside and spread around the pan. NOTE: If you are using a nonstick pan, simply preheat the oven and go to step 2.

2. In a large saucepan, mix brown sugar, water, lard or shortening, raisins, nutmeg, cinnamon, and cloves.

3. Ask an adult to help you place the saucepan on the stove top at a moderate heat, stirring often. Bring to a boil and continue to boil, stirring constantly, for 3 minutes. Remove from heat and let cool completely.

4. In a small bowl, dissolve baking soda in 2 tablespoons of water. Add this mixture and salt to saucepan. Stir.

5. In a medium bowl, mix flour and baking powder. Add mixture to saucepan. Stir to blend well.

6. Pour into pan, spreading batter out to corners. Bake 50 minutes, or until cake begins to pull away from sides of pan. It should be springy to the touch. (Ask an adult to help you check and remove finished cake from the oven.)

7. Cool cake on a wire rack. Cut into squares and serve without icing.

Serves 8 to 9

NOTE TO TEACHERS AND ADULTS

For children, the home front during World War II may seem like part of a far-off past. But there are many ways to make this era and its people come alive. Along with encouraging children to cook wartime recipes, you can explore America's World War II past in other ways. One way is to read more about the era. More books on the topic are listed on pages 45 and 46. Another way to explore the past is to train young readers to study historical photographs. Historical photographs hold many clues about how life was lived in earlier times.

Ask your children or students to look for the details and "read" all the information in each picture in this book. For example, how many different ways are children shown supporting the war effort in the photographs? To encourage young readers to learn to read historical photographs, have them try these activities:

Writing a Journal

Choose one of the children pictured in this book. From the child's perspective, or point of view, write entries for a journal that you will keep throughout World War II. To start, choose an event or activity shown in the photographs in this book, described in the text, or listed in the time line on page 48. Then write an entry that tells about what you did to take part in the activity, how you learned about the important event, and how your life is changing because of the war.

Reuse, Recycle, and Make Do

Look at the photographs in this book and write down all the things you see children collecting or gathering, either to recycle or reuse. Write down the reasons why such things were collected, if you know. Next, take a look around your home and write down all the things you and your family collect and save to recycle or reuse in the future. Write down the reasons why you collect the things. Finally, compare your lists. What kinds of things did people collect and save during World War II that people in your home don't collect? What things do you save that are the same? Are the reasons why you collect these things the same? What kinds of things would you be willing to recycle, reuse, or do without if the United States were at war?

Gathering Memories

Set aside time in the evening or on a weekend to interview a grandparent, other relative, or friend who is sixty-five years old or older. Ask this person to share his or her memories of World War II. Did he or she serve in the war? Where did he serve? What did she do? Was he or she a child on the home front? What does she remember of shortages, ration stamps, and wartime newsreels? How did the war affect his life?

If you don't know anyone who has wartime memories, take a look at the history of your town or city. Visit the local historical society and read old newspapers to find out how your town changed during World War II. Was there an army base nearby or a factory making military supplies? Were dances held in your town for soldiers? Is there a World War II memorial in your town? Are the names of servicemen and servicewomen listed on the memorial? How many people from your city served in the war? How many died in the fighting?

RESOURCES ON THE WORLD WAR II HOME FRONT

Giff, Patricia Reilly. *Lily's Crossing.* New York: Delacorte, 1997. In this novel for middle-grade readers, Lily spends the summer of 1944 in a seaside town with her grandmother while her father is in the army. There, she befriends Albert, a young Hungarian refugee.

Greenfield, Eloise. *Easter Parade.* Illustrated by Jan Spivey Gilchrist. New York: Hyperion Books for Children, 1998. Cousins Leanna and Elizabeth make preparations for the annual Easter Parade despite their worries over Elizabeth's father, who is a soldier in World War II.

Hahn, Mary Downing. *Stepping on the Cracks.* New York: Clarion Books, 1991. Margaret's and Elizabeth's brothers are fighting in World War II, but Margaret and Elizabeth are busy fighting the class bully, Gordy. The girls discover Gordy's secret and must decide whether or not to help a deserter.

Krull, Kathleen. *V Is for Victory: America Remembers World War II.* New York: Apple Soup Books/Alfred A. Knopf, 1995. This scrapbook of photos and other items shows life in America and events abroad during World War II.

Lee, Milly. *Nim and the War Effort.* Illustrated by Yangsook Choi. New York: Farrar, Straus & Giroux, 1997. This picture book tells the story of Nim, a girl in San Francisco's Chinatown in 1943, and her desire to win the school newspaper drive to help the war effort.

Reeder, Carolyn. *Foster's War.* New York: Scholastic Press, 1998. In this novel for middle-grade readers, Foster's brother Mel is in the army and his best friend, who is Japanese, is sent to an internment camp.

Salisbury, Graham. *Under the Blood-Red Sun.* New York: Delacorte Press, 1994. Tomi, a boy of Japanese ancestry living in Hawaii, likes to play baseball with his friends. But when the Japanese bomb Pearl Harbor, everything changes.

Stevenson, James. *Don't You Know There's a War On?* New York: Greenwillow Books, 1992. In this humorous picture book, the author recalls his impressions of growing up in America during World War II.

Welch, Catherine A. *Children of the Relocation Camps.* Minneapolis, MN: Carolrhoda Books, Inc., 2000. Pictures and text tell of the experience of young Japanese Americans sent to relocation camps during World War II.

Whitman, Sylvia. *V Is for Victory: The Home Front in America during World War II.* Minneapolis, MN: Lerner Publications Company, 1992. This nonfiction book looks at Americans at home and how they supported the war effort.

Websites
<http://library.advanced.org/15511>
This site includes a time line of major events in World War II, historical photographs, and a simulation of family life during the war.

<http://www.corbis.com/scripts/FDRscrpt/ww2.pl?1+4+1+0+0>
View photographs from the Corbis collection depicting the lives of women and children in America during World War II.

New Words

Allies: the team of the United States, Britain, France, and Russia during World War II

ancestry: family background

assembly line: a line of workers making things in a factory

atomic bomb: a very powerful explosive made by splitting tiny particles called atoms

draft: to require people to serve in the military

home front: in a country at war, the places where nonmilitary men, women, and children live and work

newsreels: short films that report news

radiation: rays of light or heat, often dangerous

ration: a system of distributing scarce food and other items

suburbs: areas outside a city

veterans: people who have served in the military in the past

Index

Time Line

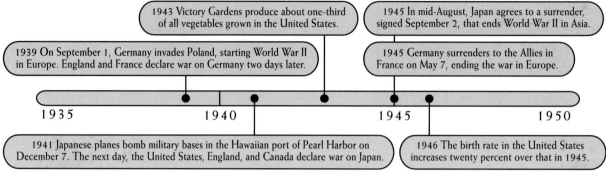

1943 Victory Gardens produce about one-third of all vegetables grown in the United States.

1945 In mid-August, Japan agrees to a surrender, signed September 2, that ends World War II in Asia.

1939 On September 1, Germany invades Poland, starting World War II in Europe. England and France declare war on Germany two days later.

1945 Germany surrenders to the Allies in France on May 7, ending the war in Europe.

1935   1940   1945   1950

1941 Japanese planes bomb military bases in the Hawaiian port of Pearl Harbor on December 7. The next day, the United States, England, and Canada declare war on Japan.

1946 The birth rate in the United States increases twenty percent over that in 1945.

About the Author

Sylvia Whitman lives with her husband and daughter in Orlando, Florida, and coordinates the writing center at Rollins College. She has degrees in folklore and mythology, American studies, and creative writing. Her publications for children include a half dozen history books.

"My parents met and married during World War II," she says. "My mom was an amateur pilot, but since women weren't allowed to fly over the ocean, she worked briefly as an observer mapping landmarks from the air. Just out of college, my dad joined the navy, training, teaching, and serving on ships. My parents say they had forty-two addresses during the war!"

Acknowledgments

Minnesota Historical Society, front cover, pp. 12, 16; Franklin D. Roosevelt, back cover [NLR-PHOCO-65702(40)], pp. 5 [NLR-PHOCO-66131(37)], 6 [NLR-PHOCO-53227(1657)], 20 [NLR-PHOCO-6798(10)], 21 [NLR-PHOCO-65757(10)], 24 [NLR-PHOCO-66158(6)], 25 [NLR-PHOCO-66158(10)], 26 [NLR-PHOCO-66298(8)], 27 [NLR-PHOCO-66178(6)], 28 [NLR-PHOCO-65701(31)], 29 [NLR-PHOCO-65701(36)], 31 [NLR-PHOCO-66297(4)], 37 [NLR-PHOCO-53227(2071)]; National Archives, pp. 1 [W&C 792], 2 [NWDNS-208-NP-4FFF-1], 7 [NWDNS-210-G-A78], 10 [NWDNS-208-NP-3KK-1], 11 [NWDNS-208-NP-4W-3], 13 [NWDNS-210-G-C519], 14 [NWDNS-210-G-2-C423], 15 [NWDNS-210-G-2-C767], 17 [NWDNS-208-AA-2F-20], 19 [W&C 791], 23 [NWDNS-208-NP-3MM-1], 30 [NWDNS-210-G-E964], 33 [NWDNS-80-G-377554], 35 [NWDNS-208-N-43888], 36 [NWDNS-111-SC-329414], 38 [NWDNS-245-MS-153USN]; National Archives Pacific Region, p. 8 [NRHS-21-DCHI-HIHC-HC298-298REXH14(5)]; Anthony Potter Collection/Archive Photos, p. 9; © Bettman/CORBIS, pp. 18, 32; Minneapolis Public Library, Kittleson World War II Collection, p. 22; © CORBIS, p. 34; © CORBIS/Bettmann-Gendreau, p. 39.